What Child Is This?

primo

English Carol
Arr. by Kathleen Massoud

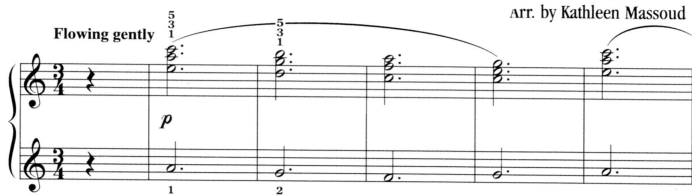

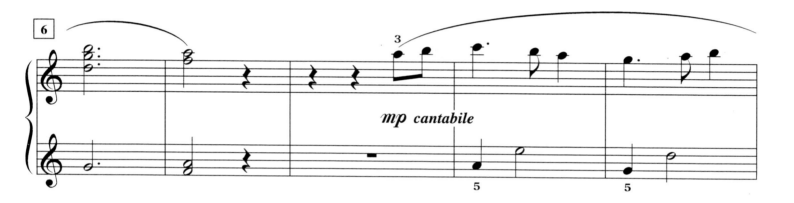

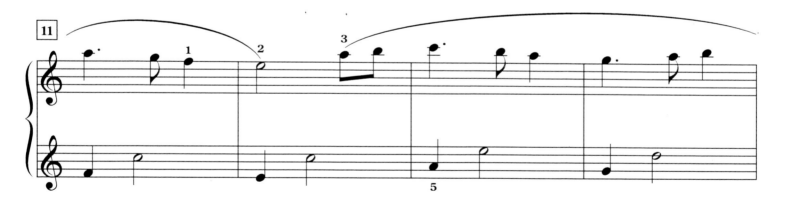

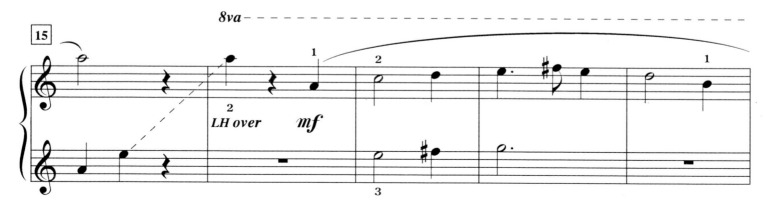

secondo

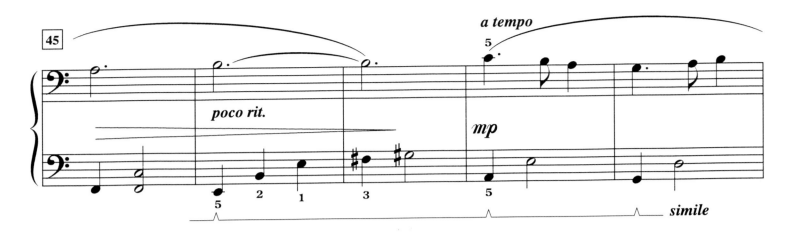

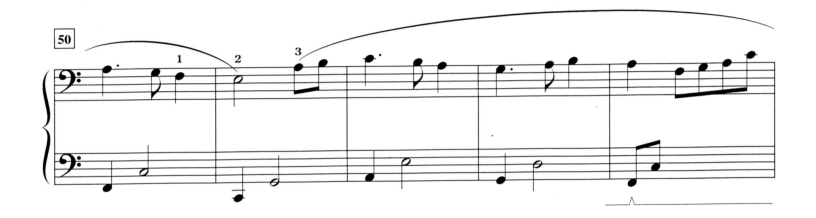

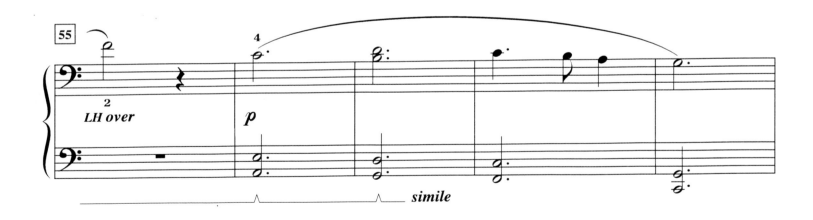

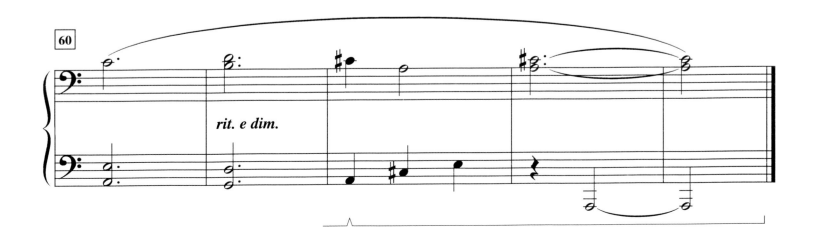

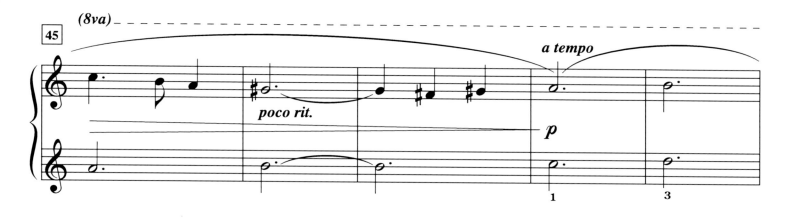

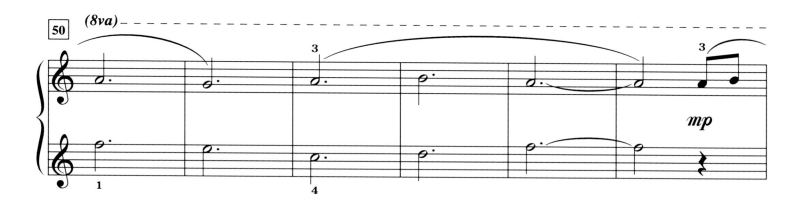

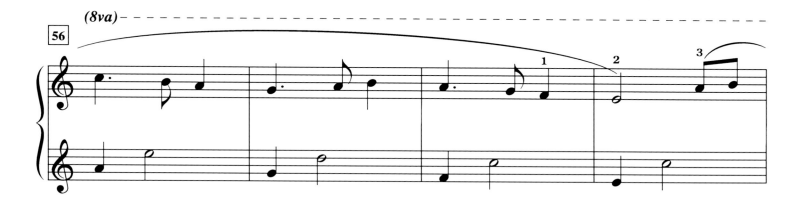

Favorite Duets from Alfred

Celebrated Piano Duets (Vandall)
These books are new compilations of favorite Vandall duets complete with new engravings with careful attention to layout.

Classics for Piano Duet (Tingley)
This series offers beginners the opportunity to play the classics. By dividing the pieces between two performers, the parts are simpler but the overall effect is rich and sparkling.

Dances for Two (Rollin)
These duets capture the essence of dance music. Book 1 includes a French waltz, a jig, a tap dance and a Baroque dance. Book 2 includes a Charleston, a polka, a Russian waltz and a rock and roll dance. Book 3 includes a paso doble, big band swing, samba, and Broadway dance.

Duet Classics for Piano (Kowalchyk/Lancaster)
These unique volumes contain duets in their original form written by composers who lived in the 18th, 19th and 20th centuries.

Duets for Animal Lovers (Goldston)
These indispensible collections add variety and help make practicing the piano become less work and more fun!

Easy Classical Piano Duets
for Teacher and Student (Kowalchyk/Lancaster)
A valuable assortment of teacher/student duets in their original form written by teachers and composers during the 18th and 19th centuries. The student parts are limited to 5-finger position and fall primarily within the grand staff reading range.

Essential Keyboard Duets
These duets provide pianists the opportunity to become familiar with a broad range of literature and to experience well-known works in a more immediate and in-depth manner.

Famous & Fun Duets (Matz)
Famous & Fun Duets offer a wonderful introduction to timeless masterpieces and audience favorites. The arrangements include themes from symphonic, operatic, and keyboard literature.

Famous & Fun Pop Duets (Matz)
This graded series contains popular hits from movies, radio, and TV. Each piece has been arranged especially for students of equal ability, while remaining faithful to the original.

First Favorite Duets (Olson)
Easy 5-finger arrangements of the world's most popular melodies, designed to encourage independent reading. Duet accompaniments provide a fuller sound.

Five-Star Duets (Alexander)
These colorful arrangements make it possible for elementary pianists to experience the joy of duet playing at the earliest opportunity. Both primo and secondo feature the melody and are equal in difficulty.

Grand Duets for Piano (Bober)
The thrill of making music with a friend or teacher is captured in this new series of duets. A variety of keys, styles, meters, and tempos are featured.

Jazz, Rags & Blues for Two (Mier)
The magic of Martha Mier's Jazz, Rags & Blues is back in this series—Jazz, Rags & Blues for Two. Enjoy the syncopated rhythms, colorful sounds, and rich harmonies of jazz in a variety of styles.

Just for Two (Alexander)
The solo piano series, Just for You, was one of Dennis Alexander's first and best-selling series with Alfred. In Just for Two, Dennis has created duet versions of many favorites from each book of the original series. Students will enjoy making music together with these duets that are "twice the fun" as the originals.

Just for You & Me (Alexander)
Syncopation, singing melodies, tender ballads, mixed meters, and mellow contemporary sounds are all found in this collection, designed to provide hours of musical enjoyment.

Kaleidoscope Duets (George)
These books introduce the student to a wide variety of musical designs and colors that spark the imagination while developing technical skills.

Masterwork Classics Duets (Kowalchyk/Lancaster/Magrath)
These graded collections of piano duets by master composers are among the best literature available at respective levels. Each duet, written by composers who lived in the 18th, 19th and 20th century, has been carefully edited and fingered for performance ease.

Music for Sharing (Goldston)
The wide variety of styles presented in these books are perfect for recitals, sight-reading or just for fun!

Terrific Tunes for Two (Mier)
The duets in Terrific Tunes for Two will encourage students to play with imagination. Both the primo and secondo parts are written at an equal level of difficulty.

Treasures for Two (Mier)
These two volumes each contain 6 captivating duets in various styles including blues, jazz, ragtime, and even a tango. Both the primo and secondo parts are written at the same level of difficulty.

18975 $4.99 in USA

ISBN 0-7390-0370-4

ISBN-10: 0-7390-037?
ISBN-13: 978-0-7390-0?

Alfred

alfred.com

Christmas Rhapsody
Recital Medley for Intermediate Pianists

Wesley Schaum

Christmas Rhapsody
Recital Medley for Intermediate Pianists

Arr. Wesley Schaum